A Day in the Life of a...

Postman

Carol Watson

Watts Books

London ● New York ● Sydney

It's five o'clock in the morning and Basra arrives at work. He is a postman at a large delivery office.

"Morning, Basra!" say the others. All the postmen are beginning to sort out the large sacks of mail that have arrived.

Basra begins
to collect the
post that is for
his 'walk'.
He takes it to
his delivery
frame ready
for sorting.

Then Basra begins the long job
of sorting each letter.
He puts the post in the order
he will deliver it, road by road.

Basra keeps the large packets separate from the letters. "Here's one sent to the wrong address," he says to himself.

He writes on the letter, 'Return to Sender', so that the right address can be written on it.

"There's a registered letter for you," says the clerk.

Basra signs a form and takes the letter.

He looks at the notice board for any new information about his walk.

When he
has finished
sorting,
Basra puts
elastic bands
round
each bundle
of letters.

He lays
them out
in order
ready to
put in his
pouch.

8

Then, Basra carefully and neatly
packs all the post into his
bag. The first letters to be
delivered go in the pouch last.

When everything is ready Basra
signs out of the delivery office
and writes down the time.
He gets his bicycle out of the shed.

Basra sets off. When he reaches his walk he parks the bicycle and locks it up until he needs it again.

Now he starts to deliver the letters. It's still early in the morning and most people are asleep.

"There's a lot of post for Harry Lynch, today," thinks Basra. "It must be his birthday."

Harry opens his front door. "Happy Birthday!" says Basra.

13

Basra reaches the house where he must deliver the registered letter. Someone has to sign for it, so Basra knocks on the door.

Nobody answers, so Basra puts
a form through the letterbox
saying there is a registered
letter at the post office.

At last, Basra has finished his
first delivery. It is 9.30am.
Back at the office he signs in again.
"Breakfast-time!" says Basra.

After breakfast, Basra sorts out the post for the second delivery. Then he sets out on his round again.

Basra delivers a special letter
to someone who wasn't in earlier.
"Hello, Basra," he says. "How
are you?"

It's 12.30 in the afternoon and Basra has finished his day. He puts his bicycle away. Now he can go home and rest.

Make a mailbox

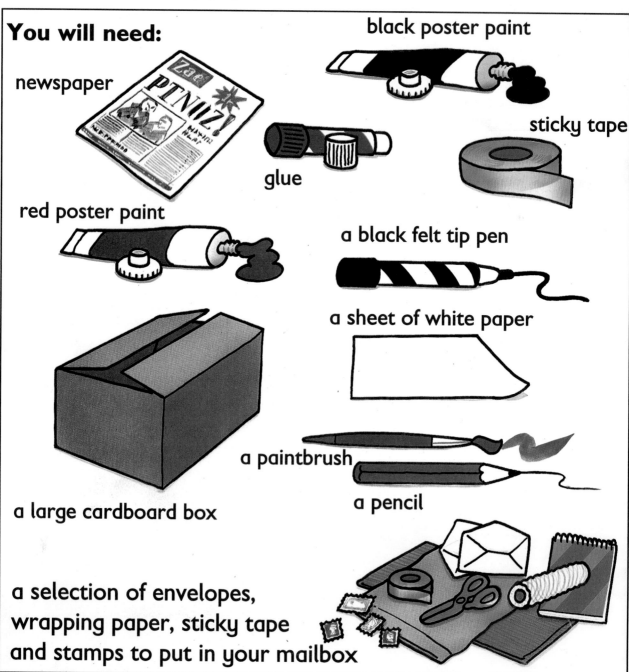

You will need:

newspaper

black poster paint

glue

sticky tape

red poster paint

a black felt tip pen

a sheet of white paper

a large cardboard box

a paintbrush

a pencil

a selection of envelopes, wrapping paper, sticky tape and stamps to put in your mailbox

1. Tuck the top flaps of the box inside. Cover the floor or table with newspaper. Put your box on it and paint it red.

2. When the red paint is completely dry, use a pencil to mark out the word 'MAILBOX' along the side of your box.

3. Carefully paint over the pencil outline with black paint.

4. Now fill your mailbox with everything you will need.

21

How you can help the Post Office

1. Always address your letters properly.

2. If you don't know the postcode, ring the Postcode Enquiry Line (0345 111222).

3. If you are sending a packet or parcel make sure you seal it up properly. Wrap fragile things in plenty of padding. Write FRAGILE or HANDLE WITH CARE on the outside of the parcel.

4. If you use staples to seal up your packet, cover the stapled end with sticky tape on both sides.

5. If you are posting a lot of letters or cards at the same time, put them in bundles with elastic bands.

Facts about the Post Office

The Post Office Corporation is made up of three separate businesses: Royal Mail, Parcel Force and Post Office Counters Ltd.

The Royal Mail deals with over 60 million letters and packets a day. It delivers mail to about 24 million addresses in all parts of the United Kingdom from Monday to Saturday.

First Class post is delivered on the next working day after collection, and Second Class post by the third working day. If there is not enough payment on a First Class letter, it will automatically go Second Class.

If your letter, packet or parcel is urgent or valuable, you can choose special ways of sending it:-

1. Special Delivery - This gets your post there the next day before 12.30pm.

2. Recorded Delivery - This has to be signed for when delivered so there is proof the letter has arrived.

3. Registered and Registered Plus - This guarantees your post arrives at its destination the next day. It has to be signed for as proof of delivery. If the letter or packet gets lost or is damaged, you can receive up to £2,200 in compensation.

23

Index

©1996 Watts Books

Watts Books
96 Leonard Street
London EC2A 4RH

Franklin Watts Australia
14 Mars Road
Lane Cove
NSW 2066

UK ISBN: 0 7496 2333 0

Dewey Decimal
Classification Number 383

10 9 8 7 6 5 4 3 2 1

A CIP catalogue record for
this book is available from
the British Library.

Printed in Malaysia

Editor: Sarah Ridley
Designer: Nina Kingsbury
Photographer: Chris Honeywell
Illustrator: Sean Wilkinson

With thanks to: Mr Doug Frankham,
Delivery Office Manager, Mr Basra and
other members of Hounslow Delivery Office;
Harry Lynch, Mr Al Senussi Abed and Mr
George Andreas.